W9-BVZ-238

WITHDRAWN

THE LIBRARY OF
AMERICAN
LIVES AND TIMES™

BENJAMIN FRANKLIN

Inventor, Writer, and Patriot

Ryan P. Randolph

The Rosen Publishing Group's
PowerPlus Books™
New York

For my dad, William Randolph, with love

Published in 2003 by The Rosen Publishing Group, Inc.
29 East 21st Street, New York, NY 10010

First Edition

*Editor's Note: All quotations have been reproduced as they appeared in
the letters and diaries from which they were borrowed. No correction was
made to the inconsistent spelling that was common in that time period.*

Library of Congress Cataloging-in-Publication Data

Randolph, Ryan P.
Benjamin Franklin : inventor, writer, patriot / by Ryan P. Randolph.
   p. cm. — (The library of American lives and times)
 ISBN 0-8239-5751-9
1. Franklin, Benjamin, 1706–1790—Juvenile literature. 2. Statesmen—
United States—Biography—Juvenile literature. 3. Scientists—United
States—Biography—Juvenile literature. 4. Inventors—United States —
Biography—Juvenile literature. 5. Printers—United States—
Biography— Juvenile literature. [1. Franklin, Benjamin, 1706–1790. 2.
Statesmen. 3. Scientists. 4. Inventors. 5. Printers.] I. Title. II. Series.
 E302.6.F8 R19 2003
 973.3'092—dc21

                                        2001005542

Manufactured in the United States of America

CONTENTS

1. An Introduction to Benjamin Franklin

A life as full of history and achievements as the life of Benjamin Franklin is hard to fit into one book. This difficulty is because he was known in so many ways: as a scientist, a philosopher, a writer, an inventor, a politician, a businessman, a moralist, and a diplomat. The son of a Boston soap- and candle-maker, Franklin would grow up to be the most famous American of his time, and perhaps one of the most famous Americans of any time.

Franklin, born in 1706, was one of the principal American patriots and the key diplomat and statesman for the Americans during the American Revolution. Even before the American Revolution, he was the best-known American in Europe because of his fame as a scientist, an inventor, and a writer.

Much is known about Franklin through his writings. They are the volumes of letters that he wrote to friends and the writings in his famous *Poor Richard's*

This portrait of Benjamin Franklin was painted by Joseph-Siffred Duplessis. Franklin (1706–1790), a man of many talents and interests, is best remembered as an American patriot and diplomat.

Almanack, as well as his pamphlets and articles promoting various causes or ideas. There is also his autobiography, Franklin's own account of his life. Franklin wrote this autobiography in four segments toward the end of his life, starting the first part in 1771, and finishing the last part in 1788. Much of what we know about Franklin comes from *The Autobiography of Benjamin Franklin*. It is one of the most-read autobiographies in the world.

Franklin is sometimes criticized for being arrogant, or less humble than his writings would indicate. In fact, his autobiography contains passages that sound humble but actually reveal him to be self-centered. Despite his many great contributions to society, at times, as a scientist and a thinker, he made conclusions that were wrong, as do many scientists. Although some criticism of Franklin is justified, some of it comes from jealousy of his worldwide fame and his association with some of the greatest minds of the time.

Franklin is known for his contributions as an inventor and a scientist. He invented an efficient, safe stove for colonial homes, bifocals to improve people's eyesight, a popular musical instrument called the armonica, and lightning rods to protect buildings. Franklin was also the first to map the Gulf Stream current in the Atlantic Ocean. Franklin's most well known experiments advanced the study of electricity by many years. Most people have heard of one famous experiment,

Benjamin Franklin invented bifocals, or glasses that would allow people to see both near and far. He had two pairs of spectacles cut in half and put half of each lens in a single frame. A reproduction of bifocals designed by Franklin in 1785 *(above)* is on display at the Franklin Institute Science Museum in Philadelphia.

during which Franklin was shocked by lightning while flying a kite with a metal key attached to it during a storm.

Besides his advances in the study of electricity, Franklin was involved in founding a hospital, a police watch, fire companies, and a library in Philadelphia.

As postmaster general of the colonies, Franklin modernized the way that mail and post offices operated. He was also involved in the founding of what would become the University of Pennsylvania, and he

Benjamin Franklin believed in the pursuit of knowledge by all people. In January 1751, his idea for a Pennsylvania academy became a reality. Today we know Franklin's academy as the University of Pennsylvania. This is an 1842 colored lithograph by John Casper Wild depicting the University of Pennsylvania.

played a vital role in raising money for and in organizing the Pennsylvania militia.

Franklin's civic duties were not limited to the American city of Philadelphia or to colonial Pennsylvania. He became the greatest supporter of colonial rights in London. The American Revolution started when America's thirteen colonies and Britain failed to agree on the rights the colonists should have, and the taxes they should pay. During the war, Franklin was instrumental in working to get France to give money to the Continental army and eventually to join with the American colonies against Britain. After America won the war, Franklin served on the diplomatic team that negotiated and signed the Treaty of Paris. In the treaty, Britain recognized the independence of the American colonies.

Toward the end of his life, Franklin returned to his home in Philadelphia, where he was elected president of Pennsylvania. In this role, Franklin served as a moderator and a mentor in the creation of the U.S. Constitution. Along with George Washington, Franklin

The signing of the Declaration of Independence is depicted in this historical painting by John Trumbull, which he painted around 1817. Franklin not only signed the Declaration of Independence but also helped to write it. This historic document declared the freedom and the independence of the thirteen American colonies from Britain.

was one of the most famous and important delegates at the convention. Through his fame both in America and around the globe, as well as through his role in the American Revolution and the founding of the nation, Franklin was one of the most influential founding fathers of the United States.

Franklin's intelligence, wisdom, curiosity, and abilities won him many more friends and admirers than critics. Considering all Franklin's achievements, it is no wonder that Franklin is such an important figure in history.

2. Franklin's Boston Background

Benjamin Franklin's father, Josiah Franklin, left Britain in 1683, for a new life in Britain's American colonies. Josiah Franklin settled in Boston, where he became a tallow chandler and soap boiler. In this trade, he made and sold candles and soap. Josiah Franklin could also practice his Puritan beliefs in the strongly Puritan town of Boston. The same Puritan beliefs that drew Josiah Franklin to Boston would later drive his son Benjamin Franklin from the strictly religious city.

As with most tradesmen of his time, little is known about Josiah Franklin, because he did not write letters often or keep other records of his life. Later, in his autobiography, Benjamin Franklin remembered his father as "Well set and very strong. He was ingenious, could draw prettily, was skill'd a little in music and had a clear and pleasing voice. . . . He had mechanical genius

---

Following page: This map shows the original outline of Boston, Massachusetts, as it appeared in 1722. Benjamin Franklin was born in Boston on January 17, 1706, but would spend most of his life in Philadelphia, with occasional stays in England and France.

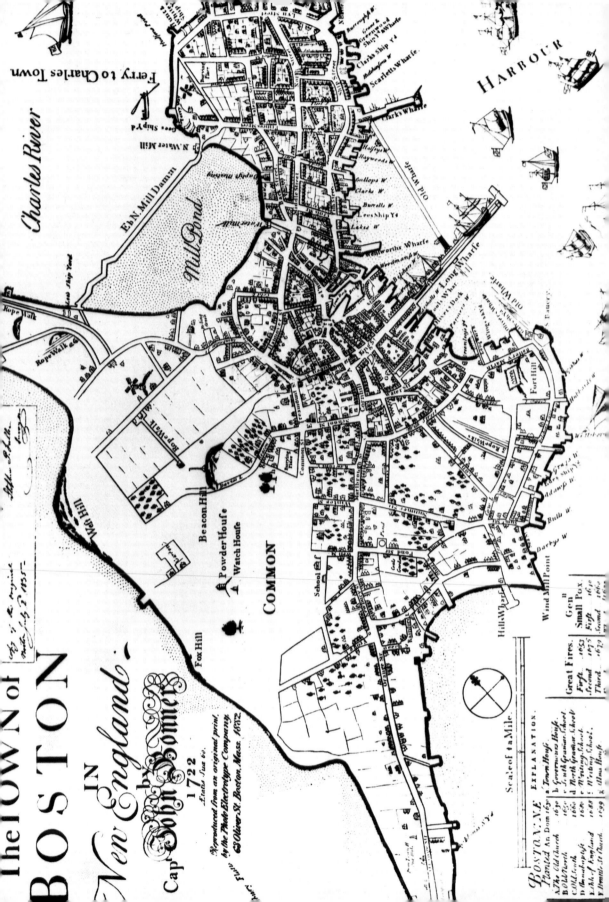

The TOWN of BOSTON
IN
New England
by
Capt. John Bonner
1722

Actual Size 60.

Reproduced from an original print
by the Photo Electrotype Company
60 Oliver St. Boston, Mass. 1902.

Charles River

Ferry to Charles Town

HARBOUR

COMMON

Beacon Hill
Powder House
Watch House

Fox Hill

Wch Hill

Rope Walk
Rope Walk

Mill Pond

Eb.N.Mill Damm

N.W.Water Mill

Long Wharfe

Old Wharfe

Fort Hill

Wind Mill Point

School

Scale of a Mile

BOSTON. EXPLANATION.
Printed An. Dom. 1722.

A The Old Church
B Old North
C Old South
D New North
E New Brick
F Church of England
G Friends Meeting H. 1699
K French Ch. Church

a Town House
b Government House
c South Grammar School
d North Grammar School
e Writing School
f Writing School
g Writing School
k Alms House

Great Fires.	Small Pox
First 1653	First 1649
Second 1675	Fifth 1678
Third 1679	Second 1666

This engraving, which was printed in Denis Diderot's encyclopedia, shows the inside of a candle-making shop. Benjamin Franklin, at age ten, was sent to work at his father's soap and candle shop. The child's main duties were cutting wicks and melting tallow, a kind of animal fat that is used to make candles.

too, and on occasion was very handy in the use of other tradesmen's tools."

Josiah Franklin had seven children with his first wife, Anne. Unfortunately, Anne died after the birth of her last child. Josiah Franklin remarried that same year to Abiah Folger, the daughter of a Puritan family from Nantucket, Massachusetts. Abiah and Josiah had ten children together. Benjamin Franklin was the fifteenth of Josiah Franklin's seventeen children. Benjamin was born on January 17, 1706, in Boston at his family's house on Milk Street. The house was close to Old South Church, where Ben Franklin was likely baptized on the same day he was born.

With the many brothers and sisters that Ben Franklin had, the house on Milk Street must have been very crowded. Growing up with so many brothers and sisters who were bigger than he was probably taught young Ben Franklin a lot about dealing with different people by using his mind, rather than by using force.

Even at a young age, Ben Franklin was interested in learning, and he recalled, "I do not remember when I

Boston Grammar School, the first public school in America, was established in 1635. At first classes were taught at the schoolmaster's house. In 1645, the school was moved to the building shown above. Benjamin Franklin was one of the children who studied there.

could not read." In 1714, an eight-year-old Franklin was sent to the Boston Grammar School. This school, known today as Boston Latin, is still in operation. Josiah Franklin wanted his son Ben to be a clergyman.

Unfortunately, Josiah could not afford the Boston Grammar School for very long, and Ben Franklin was soon sent to George Brownell's school for writing and arithmetic for one more year of schooling before starting a job. Franklin became an apprentice to his father, a candle- and soap-maker, at the age of ten. Franklin helped his father with "Cutting wick for candles, filling the dripping mold and molds for cast candles, attending to shop, going of errands, etc."

Of his new job, Franklin recalled, "I disliked the trade, and had a strong inclination for the sea, but my father declared against it." Instead Franklin's father introduced Franklin to other trades. "He therefore sometimes took me to walk with him, and see joiners, bricklayers, turners, braziers, etc." Franklin worked with his uncle as a cutler, or maker of knives, for a while. This job did not work out either because Franklin did not care for it.

Franklin liked to read. He read works by Cotton Mather, Daniel Defoe, and Jonathan Swift, among many others that students in America still read today. "This bookish inclination at length determined my father to make me a printer. . . . In 1717 my brother James returned from England with a press and letters

In his autobiography, Franklin described how he and some of his friends got into trouble, or "scrapes," as Franklin called them. There was a salt marsh where Franklin and his friends used to fish. Soon the area became too muddy in which to fish. Franklin, a leader at an early age, encouraged his friends to build a small wharf by piling up stones from a nearby construction site. As Franklin described, "Accordingly, in the Evening when the Workmen were gone, I assembled a Number of my Playfellows, and working with them diligently . . . sometimes two or three to a Stone, we brought them all away and built our little Wharf." The next day, when the workmen discovered the missing stones, Franklin and his friends were caught and got in trouble with their fathers. Franklin was a moralist, and, as with many stories, in this one he left us with this moral: "And tho' I pleaded the Usefullness of the Work, [my father] convinc'd me that nothing was useful which was not honest."

to set up his business in Boston." To prevent young Ben Franklin from going to sea, Josiah Franklin apprenticed Ben to his brother James.

James was going to start his own printing business in Boston, and Ben Franklin became his apprentice in 1718, at the age of 12. Franklin had finally found a profession he enjoyed, and he turned out to be very good at it. Ben Franklin continued to read the works of famous philosophers and essay-ists. Franklin also learned to write effectively. As Ben Franklin said, "Prose writing has been of great use to me in the course of my life, and was a principal means of my advancement."

James Franklin started his own newspaper in 1721. It was called the

Benjamin Franklin wanted to buy books, but he did not have a lot of money. He learned how to be frugal, or careful with his money, so that he could save his earnings. To do this, Franklin changed his diet to one of mostly bread, vegetables, and water. By cutting out expen-sive items such as meat and alcoholic drinks, Benjamin Franklin could save half of the money he earned to buy books.

This engraving of a print shop is from Denis Diderot's encyclopedia of trades. To the left, one worker spreads out paper, while his companion inks the type. The other workers have the job of scrutinizing each sheet for even inking and printing as it emerges from the press. Ben Franklin, at twelve, became an apprentice at his brother James's printing business.

New-England Courant. This would be Ben Franklin's first chance to write for the public. Franklin, now thirteen, knew that James thought he was too young to write for the paper. To get around this, Franklin began writing under anonymous names in 1722, and left his work under the door of the print shop. The articles were by a character he created named Mrs. Silence Dogood. This character was supposed to be a widowed woman who wrote letters to the *New-England Courant* on various subjects.

[Nº 37

THE
New-England Courant.

From MONDAY April 9. to MONDAY April 16. 1722.

To the Author of the New-England Courant.

SIR, [No 2]

ISTORIES of Lives are seldom entertaining, unless they contain something either admirable or exemplar: And since there is little or nothing of this Nature in my own Adventures, I will not tire your Readers with tedious Particulars of no Consequence, but will briefly, and in as few Words as possible, relate the most material Occurrences of my Life, and according to my Promise, confine all to this Letter.

MY Reverend Master who had hitherto remained a Batchelor, (after much Meditation on the Eighteenth verse of the Second Chapter of Genesis,) took up a Resolution to marry; and having made several unsuccessful fruitless Attempts on the more topping Sort of our Sex, and being tir'd with making troublesome Journeys and Visits to no Purpose, he began unexpectedly to cast a loving Eye upon Me, whom he had brought up cleverly to his Hand.

THERE is certainly scarce any Part of a Man's Life in which he appears more silly and ridiculous, than when he makes his first Onset in Courtship. The awkward Manner in which my Master first discover'd his Intentions, made me, in spite of my Reverence to his Person, burst out into an unmannerly Laughter: However, having ask'd his Pardon, and with much ado compos'd my Countenance, I promis'd him I would take his Proposal into serious Consideration, and speedily give him an Answer.

AS he had been a great Benefactor (and in a Manner a Father to me), I could not well deny his Request, when I once perceiv'd he was in earnest. Whether it was Love, or Gratitude, or Pride, or Three that made me consent, I know not; but is certain, he found it no hard Matter, by the Help of his Rhetorick, to conquer my Heart, and persuade me to marry him.

THIS unexpected Match was very astonishing to all the Country round about, and served to furnish them with Discourse for a long Time after; some approving it, others disliking it, as they were led by their various Fancies and Inclinations.

AT present I pass away my leisure Hours in Conversation, either with my honest Neighbour Rusticus and his Family, or with the ingenious Minister of our Town, who now lodges at my House, and by whose Assistance I intend now and then to beautify my Writings with a Sentence or two in the learned Languages, which will not only be fashionable, and pleasing to those who do not understand it, but will likewise be very ornamental.

I SHALL conclude this with my own Character, which (one would think) I should be best able to give. Know then, That I am an Enemy to Vice, and a Friend to Virtue. I am one of an extensive Charity, and a great Forgiver of private Injuries: A hearty Lover of the Clergy and all good Men; and a mortal Enemy to arbitrary Government & unlimited Power. I am naturally very jealous for the Rights and Liberties of my Country; & the least appearance of an Incroachment on those invaluable Priviledges, is apt to make my Blood boil exceedingly. I have likewise a natural Inclination to observe and reprove the Faults of others, at which I have an excellent Faculty. I speak this by Way of Warning to all such whose Offences shall come under my Cognizance, for I never intend to wrap my Talent in a Napkin. To be brief; I am courteous and affable, good-humour'd (unless I am first provok'd,) and handsome, and sometimes witty, but always,

SIR,
Your Friend, and
Humble Servant,
SILENCE DOGOOD.

witty, but always,

S I R,
Your Friend, and
Humble Servant,
SILENCE DOGOOD.

by as of their Writings, I conclude, the Fury; but freely confess that I am not marry'd according to the Laws of this Province, and throw my self entirely upon your Honours: And if your Honours

---

Franklin signed this article, which ran in the
April 16, 1722, issue of the *New-England Courant*,
"Your Friend, and Humble Servant, SILENCE DOGOOD."

The writings in the *New-England Courant*, including the Silence Dogood letters, mocked the rigid, Puritan establishment in Boston and often got James in trouble with the law. One time James was arrested and a young Ben Franklin took control of the operation of the newspaper and the print shop. After his release from jail, James found out that Ben Franklin was the author of the Silence Dogood pieces. He became jealous of all the attention his little brother and apprentice received for writing the popular letters.

The combination of the rigid, Puritan way of life in Boston and the knowledge that he could write and operate a print shop better than could his brother would lead Ben Franklin to rebel and to leave Boston. After James was released from prison and again took control of the *Courant*, Franklin decided to strike out on his own.

3. An Adventurous Youth

In September 1723, at the age of seventeen, Franklin left Boston and his obligation to James and went to the city of New York. Franklin arrived there without much money and without a job. Franklin learned that the one printer in New York, William Bradford, did not have any work available. Bradford told Franklin that he had just helped his son set up a print shop in

Pierre-Michel Alix made this 1793 portrait of Benjamin, who would become one of the most famous Americans in the eighteenth century.

Next page: New York State is highlighted in red on this map, and New York City is in blue. Benjamin Franklin hoped to find work in New York after running away from his brother James.

Necouba

St. Johans Lake

Recouba R.

Chikou timi

Tadoussac

St. Lau...

Terra Basse

Haut au Mouton

Larguein

Metis

C. St. Barnabé

The Lady Mountains

GASP

High Mountains

I. Lieures
I. Coudres
C. Oys
C. Coudres

Ance Verte

C. du Bic

R. Oys

R. Charles

C. Tormente

I. Orleans

I. Oys
Rochetes

R. Sud

Lorette
Beauport

French Settlements

Quebec

St. Helens

NEW SCOTLAND

Chaudire Bay

R. S.

Miramichi R.

Treneuse

R. St. Iuan

Nakohonac

R. St. Iuan

Iemsec

Silleri

Po rt Neuf

Saut de la Chaudiere

R. St. Croix

Fort la Tou

R. de Chene

Trois Rivers

R. Puate

R. St.

A

D

Kaouinagamick Lake

OF

Spring

Lake of St. Peters

R. St. François

Penobscot R.

Machias Har.

Red Head

Passamaquadi

Pensquie
Mount
Desart

Northern Mountains

Saut de St. Louis

F. Sorel

Monreal

Monreal I.

Fort Chambly

Fort Ste. Therese

Fort la Mothe

Saco R.

Casco Bay

Mt. Desart Rock

L. Manan

C. Manan

FUNDI BAY

Long I.

L. Pas
G. Pas

Lievre R.

River of Outrouas

St. Louis Lake

Trou

Cedres

Blusson

Waterfalls or Cataracts

Champlain Lake

NEW ENGLAND

Kenebeck R.

Pescataway

L. Manan

St. Francis Lake

Long Saut

NEW YORK

Hudsons R.

Dover

Exeter

Hampton

Casco Bay

Jeffery's Bank

Seale Isle

Sturgio Isl.

Quente

la Galleta

New Albanne

Connecticut R.

Marble Head

C. Ann

Manchester

Fort Frontenac

LAKE

Massachu

Colony

Boston Town & Harbour

C. Codd

Eastham

St. Geo
Bank

IROQUOIS

Deerfield

Hadly

Springfield

Westfield

ONE

N. York

New Jersey

Conhasset Rocks

Scituate

Marshfield

Plymouth

Colo

Nantucket Shoales

N. London

Elizabeth I.

Martha's Vineyard I.

New Rose and Crown

Old Rose and Crown

Nantucket I.

PENSILVANIA

Delaware R.

LONG ISL.

Philadelphia

Monmouth

MARYLAND

Baltemore Cou.

C. May

Dellawar Bay

Cape May

Egg Harbour

Sandy Land

New Inlet

OCEAN

EASTERN

This copy of Andrew Bradford's signature was taken from a letter that he wrote to the Society of Friends. The Society of Friends is a religious group that is more commonly known as the Quakers.

Philadelphia, and that the son was looking for help because one of his workers had died.

Too proud to go back to Boston and without an income in New York, Franklin headed for Philadelphia in October 1723. Franklin describes the storm and the dangers of his journey in the *Autobiography*. In Philadelphia, Franklin found that printer Andrew Bradford had already hired a journeyman to assist him. Franklin heard that a new printer was setting up shop elsewhere in Philadelphia. He was able to find work with printer Samuel Keimer.

Franklin began to realize that Keimer did not really know how to be a printer and had poor equipment. After meeting Andrew Bradford and seeing a bit of his printing operation, Franklin understood that although Bradford knew how to run a printing press, he could neither read nor write well. It is hard to be a good printer when you are almost "illiterate," as Franklin put it. He probably thought he could do better than both of the

Benjamin Franklin recalled the following story of his trip to Philadelphia in his autobiography:

Being b'calmed of Block Island, our people set about catching cod and hauled up a great many. Hitherto I had stuck to my resolution of not eating animal food . . . I consider'd . . . the taking of fish as a kind of unprovoked murder. . . . But I had formerly been a great lover of fish, and when this came hot out of the frying-pan it smelt admirably well. I balanc'd some time between principle and inclination, till I recollected that, when the fish were opened, I saw smaller fish taken out of their stomachs; then thought I, "If you eat one another, I don't see why we mayn't eat you." So I din'd upon cod very healthily, and continued to eat with other people, only now and then returning to a vegetable diet. So convenient a thing it is to be a reasonable creature, since it enables one to find or make a reason for every thing one has a mind to do.

printers in Philadelphia, but he did not have enough money to start his own business.

Franklin settled into his role working for Keimer and began making friends with the other young journeymen of Philadelphia. People started to take notice of Franklin, because he was educated, hardworking, and thoughtful, and he had a love of books and learning. One person who took notice of this talented new citizen was the governor of Pennsylvania, William Keith.

Keith encouraged Franklin to start a print shop. Franklin and Keith planned for Franklin to go back to Boston to ask his father for money so that he could start up his own print shop. Governor Keith would provide a letter of recommendation to help persuade Franklin's father.

In April 1724, Franklin returned to Boston to try to get money for his own print shop in Philadelphia. Franklin's father heard his son's plans and wondered why Keith would write a letter of recommendation but not put his own money behind the project. Josiah Franklin was a careful man and did not think that he could afford such a risky investment, even in his own son.

This trip to Boston was Franklin's first homecoming, and, with some money in his pocket, he went to visit James at the print shop to boast about how well he was doing in Philadelphia. As Franklin put it, "This visit of mine offended him extreamly; for when my mother some time after spoke to him of a reconciliation . . . he

This oil painting of Deborah Franklin, Benjamin's wife, was
made in 1758 or 1759 by the English painter and scientist
Benjamin Wilson. Wilson copied this picture of Deborah
from a small original sent from Philadelphia. Wilson's portrait
is the only Franklin portrait to have remained in the family.

said I had insulted him in such a manner before his people that he could never forget or forgive it."

When Franklin returned to Philadelphia, he gave Governor Keith the disappointing news from Josiah Franklin. The governor suggested that Franklin travel to London to get monetary loans and printing supplies. Keith would supply his recommendations to secure the loans. Franklin could then use the money to buy printing supplies in London, as printing presses or supplies were not made in the colonies.

While Franklin was waiting to make his trip to London in the fall, he continued to work at Keimer's print

This scene showing Benjamin Franklin passing by the door of Deborah Read, his future wife, appears in two nineteenth-century books. Benjamin would spend fifteen years of their marriage, between 1758 and 1774, in Europe on business for the government.

shop. Franklin lived in the same house as the Read family, and he used his time there to court his future wife, Deborah Read. During this period, Franklin also enjoyed talking about books and poetry with some of his friends.

In November 1724, Franklin sailed for London with his friend James Ralph to get loans and equipment for a print shop back in Philadelphia. Keith had failed to write the letters of recommendation, and Franklin sailed to London without them. This was the first of Franklin's many voyages across the Atlantic Ocean. When Franklin arrived in London on Christmas Eve, he discovered that Governor Keith did not have any credit with the printers in the city.

Franklin finally realized that Governor Keith was no real help, and Franklin was forced to find a job in London. Being in one of the largest cities in the world with no money and no job would be a challenge for anybody. Franklin was resourceful and found work with a London printer. Franklin supported his friend James Ralph as the latter tried to become a poet. Eventually Ralph moved away from London and became a teacher.

Not all of Franklin's time in London was spent at work. He enjoyed going to plays and reading books with friends, as well as trying to meet ladies. In London, as

This is a 1720 map of London, England. That year, Franklin and his friend James Ralph sailed to London in hopes of starting a print shop. It was the first of Franklin's many trips across the Atlantic Ocean.

PROSPECT der KÖNIGL. HAUPT und RESIDENTZ STADT
LONDON.

in Philadelphia, his energy and his ability to talk about books, ideas, and current events helped him to meet people. These people often were educated, and sometimes were wealthy or important. Franklin met a merchant named Thomas Denham, who invited Franklin to return to Philadelphia with him and to set up a general store.

In July 1726, Franklin sailed for Philadelphia with Denham, and, upon arrival, he became a bookkeeper and a shopkeeper at Denham's store. This lasted for less than a year, for both Franklin and Denham became very ill. When Thomas Denham died in 1727, Franklin was forced to find work as a printer with Keimer again.

4. Printer and Philadelphia Citizen

Keimer offered Franklin high wages to come back to work for him. Franklin did not want to work for Keimer again, but he needed the money and accepted the job. It did not take Franklin long to figure out that he had been hired to pass along his skills as a printer to Keimer's apprentices. Once the other men knew enough about printing, Keimer could fire Franklin. Although it was an unpleasant return to Philadelphia and to the printing business, soon Franklin would enter a period in which he would become a successful printer, an enterprising businessman, a husband, and a father.

The first step toward a successful printing business was meeting one of Keimer's apprentices, Hugh Meredith. Meredith's father provided the money for them to start a business. In spring 1728, Franklin and Hugh Meredith opened their print shop in Philadelphia. Franklin's growing reputation for hard work and high-quality printing brought them a good amount of business.

To increase the print shop's revenues, or income, Franklin decided to start a newspaper in Philadelphia in the fall of 1728. Upon hearing of Franklin's plan, Keimer rushed to put his own newspaper, *The Pennsylvania Gazette*, into print in October 1728. This meant that there were now two newspapers in town, and Franklin knew he could not successfully start a third newspaper. Instead of starting his own newspaper, in February 1728, Franklin invented a character named Busy Body who published letters in Andrew Bradford's newspaper, the *American Weekly Mercury*.

This character of Franklin's wrote about gossip, politics, and other issues. Busy Body became popular, as had Franklin's former character Silence Dogood. The popular Busy Body series in Bradford's paper took readers away from Keimer's paper. Bradford's job as postmaster allowed him to see the news from outside Philadelphia before anyone else and to share it with the public first in his popular *American Weekly Mercury*. This was another reason Keimer's paper was failing. In September 1729, Franklin bought the *Pennsylvania Gazette* from Keimer for a very cheap price. The *Gazette*'s circulation grew enormously because of Franklin's lively, well-written columns, and the paper turned a handsome profit.

Ben Franklin was always willing to try new lines of business. In 1732, Franklin became the first to publish a German-language newspaper in the colonies, but it

No. 214

THE
AMERICAN

𝕎eekly 𝕄ercury,

From TUESDAY *January* 14th, to TUESDAY *January* 21th, 172⁴⁄₃.

The Writer of the first Part of our Weekly Mercury will omit his Design of pursuing his Memoirs, for the sake of the young Lady, whose Condition is described in the following Letter. But Mr. B———— says, that if Lovina, by his means, acquires her Love, he shall expect a pair of Gloves.

Mr. B————

Sir,

AS I always find, of late, the Front of your Paper employed in giving Lectures upon several Subjects, which are not only often very diverting, but always very profitable. I hope you will not deny this Letter a Place in your Mercury, since it can be prejudicial to none, and may be the preserving me from Ruin. As you always avoid Scandal and Falsity's, I am the more desirous my Case should be seen in your Paper.

Know then, I am the Daughter, and only Child, of a Gentleman of ———— Pounds a Year, and being arrived at near Twenty Years of Age, several have made their Addresses to me, but none so successful as the only Son of a Wealthy Tradesman: As he is entirely pleasing to me, I have return'd his agreeableness with a modest Civility; but my Father being biggotted to the very Name of Gentleman, and having an innate Aversion for Traders, opposes my Choice, and declares his Blood shall never be tainted by my Wedding a Machanick. This is his Principal Argument, together with his saying, If I DISOBEY I shall not INHERIT. He recommends to my Bosom an aged Gentleman of Sixty, but of a superior Fortune and ancient Family. Alas! Mr. B————, he little knows the Sweetness of the young Traders or Mechanicks Conversation, or the melting Musick of his Voice! How dull will be the Day, if I Marry the old Sire! the Light of the Sun will be tedious to me. When we are with a Person we like, the most trifling Objects can afford delight, but with him we hate the Groves have no Pleasure, and the gentle voice

to do but to spend it: And add, what else you think will lessen his over fond Opinion of Gentlemen, and encrease his Esteem for Tradesmen, which if you can do, you'll Oblige her who is,

Sir, Your Humble Servant, *Lovina.*

Madrid, (the Capital of Spain,) Sept. 21.

The Tempest we had here on the 15th was so dreadful, that we began to believe the World was at an end: The Lightning, Thunder, and furious Rain cannot be express'd; but tho' the Lightning fell on many Houses, it did no considerable Damage, except one Flash, which falling on the Church of our Lady of Constantinople, threw down a high Wall more than an Ell in Thickness, and tumbled down by its Fall a neighbouring House: The Impetuosity of its Torrent caused by the Rain that fell in Cararacts, made a most deplorable Havock in the Suburb of St. Barbara, where several Houses were thrown down, and four Persons buryed under the Ruins. All that Part of the City call'd the Old Guards was fill'd with Water to the second Story, and much mischief would have happen'd there, if the Rapidity of the Torrent had not thrown down 50 Foot of the Wall of the Garden of Castle-Roderigo, and by that Means open'd a Passage to the Flood, and saved the Lives of the Inhabitants of that Part of the City.

Madrid, Sept. 28. The King who enjoys perfect Health applies himself with great Assiduity to the Affairs of Government. The Inquisitors have got into their Hands several Persons who are accused of Judaism, among whom are said to be two or three of Quality.

Moscow, Sept. 8.

The last Advices from Derbent assure us, that Miriweys and his Council had issued Circular Letters throughout all the Provinces of Persia, enjoining his new Subjects to take Arms and come in to him, because he design'd to retake from the Czar the Towns of Terki, Derbent, and Andreof, with the ...

This is the *American Weekly Mercury* masthead from the January 14–21, 1724, issue. In this paper, Benjamin Franklin published articles under the name of Busy Body. The articles were about politics, gossip, and other issues.

failed to catch on enough in the German communities to be profitable. In 1740, Franklin tried to start another magazine for Pennsylvania. This failed because of competition from Andrew Bradford's *American Weekly Mercury*. It also was unsuccessful because, in general, the public had a low interest in magazines.

This printing press was used by Franklin and is part of the collection of the Smithsonian's National Museum of American History. Franklin used his printing press to make newspapers and other printed materials.

In 1730, Ben Franklin started working as the official printer of Pennsylvania's government. This meant that Franklin had a contract to print government documents and currency. Because Ben Franklin did good work, it helped him to win a contract printing the currency for New

Jersey. In 1736, Franklin developed a method of printing New Jersey's currency that made it harder to counterfeit or make fake copies of the money. Another new line of business that Ben Franklin attempted and at which he succeeded was the writing and printing of almanacs.

The first edition of Ben Franklin's *Poor Richard's Almanack* was published in 1732. The last one would be published

This five pound bill was printed in 1760 by Benjamin Franklin and David Hall in Philadelphia. Franklin was a supporter of printed-paper currency. People's need for paper money helped Franklin's printing business to flourish.

in 1757. Almanacs contain information on sunrises, sunsets, weather predictions, recipes, and astrology, and, in the case of Franklin's *Almanack*, bits of wit and wisdom as well. Farmers and others used these almanacs as sources of practical information, such as when to plant certain crops.

Franklin had a knack for negotiating favorable business arrangements and for working difficult situations to

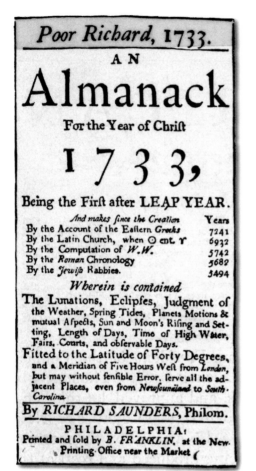

Poor Richard, 1733.

AN

Almanack

For the Year of Chrift

1733,

Being the Firft after LEAP YEAR.

And makes fince the Creation	Years
By the Account of the Eaftern *Greeks*	7241
By the Latin Church, when ☉ ent. ♈	6932
By the Computation of *W.W.*	5742
By the *Roman* Chronology	5682
By the *Jewifh* Rabbies.	5494

Wherein is contained

The Lunations, Eclipfes, Judgment of the Weather, Spring Tides, Planets Motions & mutual Afpects, Sun and Moon's Rifing and Setting, Length of Days, Time of High Water, Fairs, Courts, and obfervable Days.

Fitted to the Latitude of Forty Degrees, and a Meridian of Five Hours Weft from *London*, but may without fenfible Error, ferve all the adjacent Places, even from *Newfoundland* to *South-Carolina*

By *RICHARD SAUNDERS*, Philom.

PHILADELPHIA:

Printed and fold by *B. FRANKLIN*, at the New Printing-Office near the Market.

This is the title page of the 1733 *Poor Richard's Almanack*. Benjamin Franklin's *Almanack* was a huge bestseller. Colonists purchased about 10,000 copies each year.

his advantage. Franklin's original partner, Meredith, began to drink heavily and to develop other problems, such as losing too much money at gambling. These problems affected both his ability to do work and the reputation of the print shop. In 1730, two years after he went into business with Meredith, Franklin borrowed money from two friends and bought Hugh Meredith's share of the business. Franklin finally owned his own print shop.

Franklin also made a series of profitable partnerships with people he had trained. In these partnerships, Franklin provided money to start the shop and to buy equipment in exchange for a share of the profits for a number of years. Franklin made partnerships and sent his colleagues to South Carolina, New York, and the West Indies. The amount of money Franklin made was not as much as that made by some of the other businessmen and

Even more successful than Franklin's Poor Richard's Almanacks *are the famous quotes from them that are still around today. Many sayings found in the Almanacks are still used, though some are worded differently:*

No gains without pains.

[No pain, no gain.]

The sleeping Fox catches no poultry. Up! Up!

[The early bird catches the worm.]

Don't throw stones at your neighbors if your own windows are glass.

[People who live in glass houses should not throw stones.]

The rotten apple spoils his companion.

[One bad apple spoils the bunch.]

Some quotes are humorous analogies:

Fish and Visitors stink after three days.

A country man between two lawyers, is like a fish between two cats.

Many other quotes, whether original or not, give Franklin's view on morality and life:

Ill Customs & bad Advice are seldom forgotten.

Old Boys have their Playthings as well as young Ones: the Difference is the Price.

Necessity never made a good bargain.

Half wits talk much but say little.

Observe all men; thyself most.

Death takes no bribes.

merchants in the colonies, but it was great enough to provide him with stability.

Franklin's most significant partnership was the one he created in 1748, with David Hall, who would take control of Franklin's printing business. In 1744, Hall had come from London to work in Franklin's print shop and had proved to be very talented. After four years, in 1748, Franklin agreed that Hall would take over the day-to-day operations of the print shop. Franklin would still write for the paper and the almanac and would be a partner with Hall, but Franklin would devote more time to science and politics. He would become active in public office, serving as deputy postmaster of the colonies from 1753 to 1774.

During the time Franklin was conducting his printing business, he was also raising his young family. In September 1730, Deborah Read and Benjamin Franklin became married by common law. A common-law marriage is when two people have lived together for a long time and have shared their property because of it. Franklin and Deborah could not have a formal wedding. Deborah was still married to a man who ran away but might come back someday. Franklin had not yet had a wife before Deborah, but he did have a son, William Franklin, who was born out of wedlock. The mother of William Franklin is not known. The few enemies Benjamin Franklin made during his political career used his son's illegitimate birth to discredit Franklin.

This is a photo of the Philadelphia post office in 1775. Located on the corner of Front and Market Streets, the building had first come into use as a coffeehouse in 1754.

Franklin became the postmaster of Philadelphia in 1737, and was appointed the deputy post-master of the colonies in 1753. A post-master was responsible for the delivery of mail, which meant determining routes and methods of delivering mail, among other duties. He remained a postmaster even while he was serving in the Pennsylvania govern-ment and acting as a representative in London. As post-master, Franklin improved the mail service and developed modern techniques for mail delivery. In 1763, Franklin went on a long tour of the post offices throughout the colonies. In 1774, the British stripped Franklin of his title of postmaster, as Franklin was fighting against them. It did not matter much, because in 1775, Franklin was appointed postmaster for the rebelling colonies.

In 1732, Franklin and Deborah had their first child, Francis Folger Franklin. Unfortunately, Francis contracted smallpox and died in 1736, at age four. Franklin never forgave himself for not having his son inoculated, or protected, from smallpox. Even later in his life, Franklin wrote about Francis and mentioned to people how old his son would have been if he were alive.

It is remarkable that Franklin was able to accomplish so much outside of his busy printing press and family obligations. In 1727, Franklin had formed a discussion group with his friends, called the _Junto_. That summer, the members of this group met on Fridays to discuss books, to read aloud, and to present ideas to one another. Ben Franklin noted that "The rules that I drew up required that every member . . . should

This is a plaque for the insurance company founded by Franklin in 1752. Franklin's company was the first to make contributions toward fire prevention. It warned against fire hazards and refused to insure wooden and other buildings where the risk of fire was too great.

produce one or more queries on any point of Morals, Politics, or Natural Philosophy, to be discuss'd by the company; and once in three months read an essay of his own writing."

The number of young men in the Junto was small at first, but it grew even though membership was exclusive. The group, with Franklin as the driving force, was behind such ideas as the creation of the Library Company (founded in 1731), the Union Fire Company in Philadelphia (founded in 1736), and a city police force consisting of paid, organized night watchmen (proposed in 1736). These ideas were not new, but Franklin was able to adapt existing ideas and to put them into action in Philadelphia and in other colonies.

5. Franklin the Scientist and the Inventor

Benjamin Franklin was good at adapting ideas to benefit others. He used this skill to establish fire companies, police patrols, philosophical societies, and universities. His skill for adapting ideas to benefit people also helped him in his role as a scientist and an inventor. Franklin did not set out to become an inventor or a scientist, nor was he ever trained as a scientist or a mathematician. In fact, his theories on why things worked the way they did were not always correct. He had a natural curiosity, however, and the ability to observe and to understand how most things worked. These qualities made him a successful scientist and inventor. His practical use of his work made his contributions as an inventor and a scientist important to society.

Wishing to improve his life and the lives of those around him, Franklin was willing to share his knowledge. He demonstrated this during the winter of 1740–1741. Franklin developed a stove that burned less wood than did a regular stove, was less smoky, and heated rooms better. Ben Franklin called his invention the Pennsylvania fireplace, but others soon called it the Franklin stove, for its inventor. Pennsylvania's governor offered Franklin the right to be the only supplier of the stove in the colony, but Ben Franklin turned him down. If Franklin had not been so focused on his printing business, he could have earned a good deal of money by making and selling the efficient stoves. Instead Ben Franklin let others in the colonies profit as the suppliers of his popular invention.

Of his many inventions and discoveries, Franklin is most famous for his work with electricity. His fame in this regard is for two reasons. Franklin suggested that lightning is a form of electricity, and he developed an experiment

Franklin recalled that, one day, as a child, he was flying a kite by the Mill Pond in Boston and decided to go for a swim. While in the water, Franklin asked a friend to give him the kite and to take his clothes to the other side of the pond. When Franklin got the kite, he used it to catch the wind to pull himself to the other side of the pond with little effort and much enjoyment!

Colonial Americans used to heat their homes with their fireplaces. In the 1740s, Franklin invented an iron furnace stove that needed less wood and that was a safer way of providing heat. The Franklin stove *(above)*, also known as the Pennsylvania fireplace, is on display at the Franklin Institute Science Museum in Philadelphia.

to prove it. From these experiments, Ben Franklin also invented lightning rods. He strongly encouraged people to start using the rods to protect their wooden barns and other buildings, which could easily catch fire if struck by lightning. A lightning rod grounded a lightning bolt, or directed the electrical charge from the rod to the ground, so that there were no sparks that could ignite buildings.

In 1750, Franklin recommended the use of grounded lightning rods for "houses, ships, and even towers and churches." The practice of grounding buildings to protect them from dangerous lightning strikes is still used today.

By the time Franklin began studying electricity, it was widely thought that lightning was a form of electricity.

200	217	232	249	8	25	40	57	72	89	104	121	136	153	168	181
58	39	26	7	250	231	218	199	186	167	154	135	122	103	90	71
198	219	230	251	6	27	38	59	70	91	102	123	134	155	166	187
60	37	28	5	252	229	220	197	188	165	156	133	124	101	92	69
201	216	233	248	9	24	41	56	73	88	105	120	137	152	169	184
55	42	23	10	247	234	215	202	183	170	151	138	119	106	87	74
203	214	235	216	11	22	43	54	75	86	107	118	139	150	171	182
53	44	21	12	245	236	213	204	181	172	149	140	117	108	85	76
205	212	237	244	13	20	45	52	77	84	109	116	141	148	173	180
57	46	19	14	243	238	211	206	179	174	147	142	115	110	83	78
207	210	239	242	15	18	47	50	79	82	111	114	143	146	175	178
49	48	17	16	241	240	209	208	177	176	145	144	113	112	81	80
196	221	228	253	4	29	36	61	68	93	100	125	132	157	164	189
62	35	30	3	254	227	222	195	190	163	158	131	126	99	94	67
194	223	226	255	2	31	34	63	66	95	98	127	130	159	162	191
64	33	32	1	256	225	224	193	192	161	160	129	128	97	96	65

This drawing, printed in London in 1767, is an example of a
magic square that did not work. In ancient times,
magic squares were thought to have magical properties.

*Franklin used to amuse himself with puzzles
and brain teasers, such as magic squares.
A magic square has numbers arranged in each
box so that all rows, columns, and diagonals
add up to the same number. In a magic square
of eight, for example, each row, column, and
diagonal adds up to 260. After hearing of a
magic square of sixteen, such as the one seen here,
Franklin created his own magic square of sixteen.*

This is a wooden model of a house built in 1765, with a lightning rod on top. Buildings with lightning rods are less likely to catch on fire during a lightning storm.

In 1750, Franklin proposed an experiment to prove that the two indeed were linked. It called for placing an iron rod above a tall building during an electrical storm, or thunderstorm, to capture the lightning. Franklin was not the first person to conduct this experiment. In May 1752, using Franklin's proposed experiment, two Frenchmen successfully captured lightning and proved it to be electricity.

Franklin conducted a modified version of his own experiment, as described in the legendary story in which Benjamin Franklin flew a kite during a lightning storm. The story goes that Franklin and his son William flew the kite during a storm in June 1752. A metal key tied on the kite string was electrified by lightning. Franklin felt the shock of electricity run through him and into an electrical jar, a device that holds electricity. If it is true that Franklin conducted this experiment in June 1752, then it would have been after the Frenchmen had already successfully conducted a similar experiment. However, Franklin would not yet have heard about the Frenchmen's success.

There is some question as to whether Franklin actually conducted the kite experiment. He did not write about or tell anybody of his accomplishment right away. It was not until October 1752, that he wrote about the success of the kite experiment in *The Pennsylvania Gazette*. He barely mentioned the kite experiment in his autobiography, published in the 1770s and the 1780s. This was odd behavior for Franklin, who took care to be in touch with the scientific community and his friends about his studies in electricity. Although many believe that Franklin did conduct the experiment, they do not know the exact day or the details behind this now-famous episode.

Even if Franklin did not fly a kite during a thunderstorm that summer, his reputation as a brilliant scientist and inventor was secure. Scientists throughout Europe knew of Franklin's work, and even Louis XVI, the king of France was very impressed with Franklin. Ordinary people throughout Europe, particularly in France, also knew of him. Franklin's experiments in electricity would

In ancient times, an electrical storm, or a major storm accompanied by lightning, was looked on as a show of power by an offended god. This did not change until Benjamin Franklin had his idea that that lightning is actually an electrical spark.

It is not known for sure whether the story of Franklin's kite experiment is fact or merely legend. However, it is widely believed that in June 1752, he flew a kite in a lightning storm to prove the link between lightning and electricity. The print on the following page, created in 1876 by Currier & Ives, illustrates this scene. In the portrait, Franklin's son William assists him in raising the kite.

As one might imagine, Franklin's experiments with electricity involved considerable personal risk. Once, while attempting to kill a turkey with electricity, Franklin accidentally knocked himself unconscious. Afterward, he made a joke in reference to the event. "I meant to kill a turkey, and instead, I nearly killed a goose," he said, implying that he was the goose.

The Copley Medal is awarded each year by the Royal Society
of London for outstanding achievement in scientific research.
It is the most prestigious scientific award in Britain.

win him the important Copley Medal from the Royal
Society of London in 1753. Much like the Nobel Prize
today, the Copley Medal was the most prestigious award
that a scientist could receive for discoveries he had made.
During his lifetime, Franklin would gain honorary master's degrees and doctorates from many universities in
the colonies and throughout Britain and France.

Franklin continued to provide important contributions to the study of electricity. However, he was never
able to devote as much time to it as he had when he had
just sold his printing business and was not yet heavily
involved in politics.

6. Franklin's Role in Colonial Politics

In May 1751, Benjamin Franklin was elected to the Pennsylvania assembly. Franklin, at age forty-five, basically entered a second career, in politics, which would last late into his life. He became a politician, an ambassador, a diplomat, and a statesman. Franklin began his political career as a local politician in the colony of Pennsylvania. He was defending the British Empire. Events would occur to change him into a leading voice against the British Empire. At the end of his life, Franklin was considered one of the most respected statesmen of the newly formed United States.

Before Franklin was elected to the Pennsylvania assembly, he had already gained popularity in the colony as the author of proposals for fire companies, police patrols, and education so as to improve the city of Philadelphia. Franklin also had supported the British

---

Next page: This map of North America shows the colonial possessions of Britain and France in 1755. During the eighteenth century, Britain and France fought over land in North America. Benjamin Franklin originally supported Britain in its desire to expand and take over French territory in America and Canada.

CARTE
DES POSSESSIONS
ANGLOISES & FRANÇOISES
DU CONTINENT DE
L'AMÉRIQUE SEPTENTRIONALE
1755.

Echelle.

Empire's desire to expand its claim to lands in America and in Canada. Britain gained control of Canada from France in the French and Indian War (1754–1763). The expansion into Canada would protect Pennsylvania from French attacks and from attacks by Native Americans allied with the French. Franklin even raised a volunteer militia and funds for the purchase of weapons when the Pennsylvania assembly refused to pay for them. The volunteer militia and the new weapons would be used to defend against enemy attacks.

Of all the colonies, Pennsylvania was the most unique. In 1681, the king of England, Charles II, gave a large tract of land west of New Jersey to William Penn and his family to pay off debts the government owed. The Penn family, who were residents of Britain, did not have to pay taxes on the land that they now owned in the American colony. The

William Penn was born in Britain in 1644 and spent most of his life there, but he is noted for the role he played in early American history. Penn is considered the founder of Pennsylvania.

colony of Pennsylvania could not raise the money to pay for either the soldiers or the equipment to defend itself from Native American and French attacks as could the other colonies. Franklin would spend much of his early political career both in the Pennsylvania assembly and as its representative in London, trying to make the Penn family give money for the defense of the colony.

In 1754, the French and Indian War began. The British and the French were fighting each other in Europe and in the colonies. With bands of French troops and their Native American allies attacking colonial outposts, the colonists felt they needed to react. Delegates from each colony met in Albany, New York, during the summer of 1754 to confirm their alliance with the Iroquois Confederacy of Indian tribes. Colonists hoped that an alliance with these Native American nations would protect colonial settlements from Native American attacks.

In Albany the colonists, led by Franklin and Thomas Hutchinson—a future governor of Massachusetts—also discussed a union of colonies. The tribes of the Iroquois Confederacy were independent but worked together to protect all of their interests. Franklin and Hutchinson observed this and drafted an important plan that proposed to unify the colonies into a confederation under the British Empire. The proposal was rejected by many colonies, including Pennsylvania, and by the British government. Many of the ideas for the Articles of

Benjamin Franklin's political cartoon, entitled *Join, or Die*, appeared in Franklin's *The Pennsylvania Gazette* on May 9, 1754. Franklin's cartoon reflected his political conviction that the colonies needed to unite. The cartoon was commonly used as a newspaper heading in 1776.

The Albany meeting inspired Franklin to create and to publish what is considered the first political cartoon in America: a snake cut into pieces representing the separate colonies with the title Join, or Die. *The purpose of the cartoon was to warn colonists about the French threat to the western colonial settlements. The idea was that a unified group of colonies could better defend themselves against this threat.*

Confederation and the U.S. Constitution were influenced by the historic meeting in Albany in 1754, and the ideas for a colonial union that came from it.

Just because the plan for colonial union was rejected did not mean that Franklin gave up the cause of colonial defense and union. In fact, from 1755 to 1757, Franklin worked very hard to raise money for the British army and for Pennsylvania's own militia forces. In early 1755, Franklin went directly to the people of Pennsylvania to raise money for wagons and for equipment to supply General Edward Braddock's force of British soldiers in their fight against the French. Unfortunately, Braddock's attack on the French at Fort Duquesne in the Pennsylvania frontier turned out to be a failure.

In November 1755, the Pennsylvania assembly finally agreed to give more money to frontier defenses. Franklin then traveled to the frontier and took charge of organizing the defenses and supervising construction of a series of forts in Pennsylvania's frontier.

Franklin also continued to lead the effort to make the Penn family pay taxes on their land. A majority of members in the Pennsylvania assembly agreed with Franklin, and they selected him to petition the king and Parliament in Britain for the taxation of the Penn lands. Franklin made his second trip to London in 1757. He had a reputation as a famous scientist and philosopher. Nonetheless, this was his first trip into the politics of the capital of the British Empire, and his popularity in the colonies and among the scientific community did not count for much in the area of politics. From this point forward, Franklin would spend most of his time away from home.

Franklin was able to argue his case with British government ministers in London and with the Penn family in 1757. The issues of taxation and the rights of Pennsylvania colonists often got confused with the fact that Thomas Penn and Benjamin Franklin did not like each other. A year after Franklin arrived in London, the Penn family sent back complaints about Franklin to the Pennsylvania assembly.

It took until 1760 for the Penn family to agree to pay taxes on their lands. It is interesting to note that, although Franklin succeeded in getting the Penns to pay taxes, the fact that the government in London decided on the matter meant that the Pennsylvania assembly was not free to make its own laws.

Franklin's duties in London as a representative of the Pennsylvania assembly diminished after 1760. In 1762, Franklin and his son William were in London when George III was made the king of Britain. William Franklin had spent much of his life as a soldier and an assistant to his father. In 1762, William Franklin was appointed the governor of New Jersey. In the same year, Benjamin Franklin made the journey from London to Philadelphia and his home.

This portrait of Benjamin Franklin's son William was painted by Mather Brown in about 1790. William remained loyal to the king of Britain, George III, even though Benjamin Franklin supported American independence. Benjamin never forgave his son for remaining loyal to Britain.

Soon after his return home to Philadelphia, Franklin again turned his attention to fighting the rule of the Penn family. That the Penn family agreed to pay some taxes on their lands was not enough to satisfy Franklin. The Penn family still appointed the governor of Pennsylvania and had relative control of the colony. Franklin and his allies decided that the best course of action was to petition the king directly for the end of control of Pennsylvania by the Penn family.

Franklin wrote a pamphlet that called for the end of proprietary rule, entitled *Cool Thoughts on the Present*

Situation of Our Public Affairs, 1764. This pamphlet and Franklin's appointment as the speaker of the Pennsylvania assembly made Franklin a political target for the Penn family and their supporters.

The elections of 1764 were filled with name-calling, much of it directed at Franklin. He was accused of acting against the Penns out of his desire to be the governor of Pennsylvania. The fact that his son William was born out of wedlock was used against him. Franklin lost his place in the Pennsylvania assembly. Despite this loss, Franklin was sent back to London in 1764, to assist in petitioning the end of the Penn family's control of Pennsylvania.

7. The Coming Revolution

Franklin concentrated on removing the Penn family from power in Pennsylvania. He favored the direct rule of the British king and government instead. What Franklin failed to recognize was the undercurrent of rising resentment against the British government. This feeling among the colonists would soon develop into calls for full independence that would lead to the American Revolution in 1775. Franklin was late to embrace the cause of independence for the colonies. Like many colonists, originally he did not want to break away from Britain. Franklin was very active in trying to find a solution to the differences between the colonies and the British government.

The end of the French and Indian War marked the beginning of many colonists' antigovernment feeling. This feeling was triggered by the British government policies that would make the colonies pay for part of the war. The British government's unpopularity among colonists grew for another reason. The British tried to make sure that the colonists did not lead them into another conflict by

This 1782 portrait of Franklin was painted by Joseph Wright.
Franklin at first intended just to enlist political support for various
causes, but politics soon engulfed him. Elected to the Pennsylvania
assembly in 1751, he spent nearly forty years as a public official.

spreading into French and Native American lands in America's frontier.

In 1764, the British government passed the Sugar Act in the colonies to help pay for the war the government had fought. The Sugar Act actually reduced the tax on molasses from the West Indies that merchants in Boston and other colonies transported. The problem was that most of the colonial merchants had been smuggling the molasses from the West Indies and had not been paying any taxes. When the British tried to enforce the lower tax rate, it made the merchants unhappy.

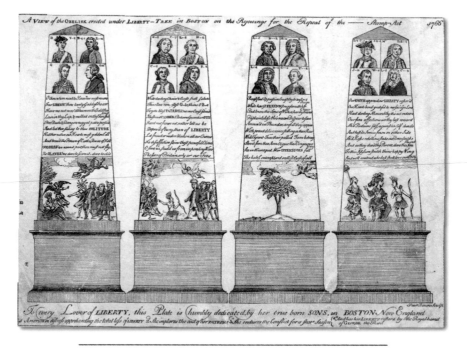

This 1766 etching by Paul Revere shows the pillar that was erected in Boston to celebrate the repeal of the Stamp Act. On each side of the pillar is a painting that portrays one phase of the struggle against the Stamp Act. Portraits are of various friends of American liberty.

Franklin returned to London in early 1765 to argue, along with other colonial agents, against Britain's proposed Stamp Act. The Stamp Act put a tax on various documents and papers. Payment of the tax was made by buying the required stamps and placing them on these papers and documents. The colonial agents argued that if the government needed money, the colonies would raise it themselves without the Stamp Act. There was no way, however, that the colonies could agree without a long debate on how much each colony would have to raise. The British government passed the Stamp Act in 1765.

As Franklin tried to adapt to the new law and to figure out how it would affect his printing partnerships, other colonists reacted violently. In the major cities such as Boston and Philadelphia, there were riots against the Stamp Act. Franklin made a major mistake by misjudging the reaction of the colonists he was representing in Pennsylvania.

The British government allowed Franklin to pick the stamp tax collector in Philadelphia. This made Franklin appear to be a supporter of the stamp tax. Riots in Philadelphia were focused on Franklin and on John Hughes, whom Franklin selected as the colony's tax collector. While Franklin was in London, his home in Philadelphia was threatened by an angry mob. His wife, Deborah, refused to leave. She and Franklin's friends convinced the mob to spare the house.

A skeleton of Benjamin Franklin's old home is displayed in Franklin Court in Philadelphia. Franklin's actual house once stood in this court. It was three stories high and had ten rooms.

The colonists' riots and protests against the Stamp Act prevented the collection of stamp taxes. In London, Franklin began arguing for the removal of the stamp taxes. The rioting in the colonies did not help Franklin convince the British government not to tax the colonies. Franklin spent almost two years making a complex argument to British prime minister George Grenville and other members of the British government.

The argument Franklin made was that colonists would not pay internal taxes, but would accept external taxes. Many in the British government asked what the difference was. After all, taxes were taxes. Franklin explained that internal taxes were on things like real estate, professions, and, of course, stamps. Franklin went on to argue that colonists were already taxed heavily on these things, and that it should be the right of the local governments to impose and to collect these taxes because that is where the colonists were represented. In reality, the colonists were taxed much more lightly than the average citizen of Britain was, and most government officials knew this.

Franklin went on to argue that the colonists would be more accepting of taxes on external goods, or items like tea, ink, or other products imported from Britain. If goods were taxed outside of the colonies, the increase in price would be blended in with the price of the goods. Franklin would find out that the logic in his argument was flawed. The colonists refused to accept any taxes from the British government.

Franklin's arguments won the day. In 1766, the Stamp Act was removed. The British government then developed an act that would place taxes on the external goods as Franklin had suggested. In 1767, the Townshend Acts duties introduced taxes on tea, lead, and ink. The colonists again rejected the taxes imposed on them by the British government. They made no distinction between internal and external taxes, which made Franklin look very bad.

The colonists thought that Franklin was helping the British government pass taxes against them. Throughout his career as a diplomat, Franklin was often the target of reports in America that he was not protecting the colonists' interests. Franklin had been working steadily to repair relations between the colonies and Britain, but he and many other colonists were finding it very hard to find a solution to the growing tensions.

The Boston Massacre happened on March 5, 1770. On this night, some British soldiers fired on a crowd of unarmed colonists who were taunting and throwing ice at them. This act provoked outrage against the British army in the colonies. Franklin continued to work in London to convince the British government to address the colonists' needs. His original job was to represent Pennsylvania in London, in 1768, but Franklin was asked to represent Georgia as well. In 1769, he was also asked to represent New Jersey. Franklin, at more than sixty years old, was not a young man. However, he was the best-known American in the world, and despite some misjudgments he had made of colonial attitudes, he was well respected in the colonies and in London. For these reasons, many colonists wanted his representation in London.

After the Boston Massacre in 1770, Franklin was also asked by the colonists to represent Massachusetts. Wills Hill, known as Lord Hillsborough, the British official in charge of American affairs at the time, initially did not allow Franklin to represent the colony, because the Massachusetts assembly did not get Governor Thomas Hutchinson's consent. The meeting showed that ministers in the British government did not believe that the people in the colonies had much power.

In 1772, Franklin secretly received letters that Massachusetts governor Hutchinson had written to his lieutenant governor, Andrew Oliver. The letters suggested that Hutchinson wanted the British government to use the British army against the colonists. Hutchinson and Franklin had worked together before, but now Hutchinson was clearly siding with the British government. Franklin decided to send the letters to Thomas Cushing, the Massachusetts speaker of the house. Franklin did so on the condition that the letters not be circulated or published. However, their content was published in the *Boston Gazette* in June 1773.

When the letters arrived in Boston in 1773, the Massachusetts assembly drafted a petition to have Hutchinson removed as governor. The petition was sent to Franklin in London. He delivered the petition for Hutchinson's removal from office to William Legge, known as Lord Dartmouth, the new minister in charge of the colonies.

Meanwhile, Hutchinson sent word of Franklin's actions to Lord Dartmouth. Franklin's actions were judged to be treason by Lord Dartmouth. He felt Franklin had betrayed the British government. This was a major offense. Franklin avoided serious danger because Thomas Cushing had destroyed the letters Franklin had sent to him, and the British government had no proof against Franklin.

This is the British East India Company seal. The company came into existence on December 31, 1600.

During this same time, events were occurring that would lead to the Boston Tea Party. In May 1773, in response to colonial protests, the British government reduced the Townshend Acts duties on most goods. However, to help out the financially troubled East India Company, the government left a small tax on tea and also lowered the price at which it could be sold. Although this may sound like it was a good deal for the colonists, it was a financial disadvantage to the merchants in the colonial port towns, who were allowed to sell only the tea belonging to the East India Company. Merchants could not sell tea they had shipped through another company. When the East India Company shipped tea to Boston in December 1773, angry colonists, dressed as Native Americans, dumped many crates of tea into Boston Harbor.

Word of the Boston Tea Party reached London in January 1774. At the same time, Franklin was told to attend a Privy Council hearing on the petition to remove Hutchinson. Instead of a meeting taking place, Franklin was put in front of a packed crowd and was accused of stealing the Hutchinson letters. The solicitor general, or the head lawyer in the British government, Alexander Wedderburn, denounced Franklin as a liar and a thief, and also used other humiliating insults. During the ordeal, Franklin refused to respond to the allegations Wedderburn made against him.

Soon after the public humiliation, Franklin was stripped of his role as deputy postmaster general for the American colonies. This event was critical in convincing Franklin that a permanent divide had grown between the American colonies and the British government.

Franklin continued struggling to find a solution between the two sides' differing views. In March 1774, Franklin was unsuccessful in preventing Parliament from passing the bill that punished Boston in response to the Tea Party. The bill closed the port and required Massachusetts to pay for the destroyed tea. Franklin made two proposals to Lord Dartmouth about how to ease the tension. Both were rejected. For the same reason, Franklin secretly met with Richard Howe, known as Lord Howe, an important British official, at Howe's sister's house to discuss possible solutions to the problems. At the beginning of 1775, Franklin worked with William

Pitt, known as the earl of Chatham, to develop a solution. William Pitt was a popular Parliament member and government minister who spoke out against British policy toward the American colonies.

In February 1775, the British government decided that the colonies must follow the laws laid down by the king and Parliament. King George III declared the colonies in rebellion against the British government. Any hope of reconciliation seemed gone. On March 20, 1775, Franklin left London for Philadelphia. The American Revolution began shortly thereafter with the Battle of Lexington and Concord, which erupted on April 19, 1775.

Amos Doolittle made this hand-colored engraving of the battle at Lexington based on eyewitness accounts that people shared with him. The sketch shows where the British and American soldiers were positioned when the first shots of the war were fired.

8. The Beginning of the Revolution

In spring 1775, Franklin returned to Philadelphia for the first time in thirteen years. The city was very different in many ways. It had grown since he left for London. His wife Deborah had passed away a year earlier, while he was in England. Franklin was not alone, though. His daughter, Sarah, her husband, Richard Bache, and several of Franklin's grandchildren lived with him.

Upon arrival in Philadelphia, Franklin was immediately made a representative of Pennsylvania in the Continental Congress, which was currently meeting in the city. Even at his advanced age, Franklin continued to be very involved in the politics of Pennsylvania and in the Continental Congress. Franklin's younger colleagues in the Continental Congress noticed that the illustrious Benjamin Franklin did not speak much publicly, but that he served on many committees. In these committees and to private individuals he offered advice, ideas, and suggestions.

For years Franklin had been criticized for being too close to the British government in his attempts to reconcile the differences between it and the colonists. After his rough experiences in London and the beginning of the American Revolution, Franklin strongly backed independence for the colonies. Franklin actively wrote essays and songs that encouraged independence and the war effort.

Franklin was very active in the Continental Congress and the Pennsylvania assembly in 1775. In July 1775, Franklin wrote a draft of the Articles of Confederation that declared the colonies independent and set up rules for governing the united colonies. Franklin's proposal was not approved by Congress, but it started the group thinking about how colonists could work together to achieve independence.

Franklin was on the committee to create a paper currency for the colonies. He had served in the British government as a postmaster general for the colonies, but now he was made postmaster general of a new post office run by the Continental Congress. He organized a mail delivery system that operated alongside the existing postal system, which was controlled by the British government.

Franklin was also involved in creating the rules and policies of the Continental army. In October, Franklin and some fellow delegates traveled to Boston, where General George Washington had joined the attack on the British army troops holding Boston. There the men developed the structure and the policies of the

This woodcut of a postrider on horseback, with bags behind him for carrying the mail, appeared on a circular issued by Benjamin Franklin in 1775. The woodcut is believed to have inspired the official seal used by the Post Office Department from 1837 to 1970.

Continental army. Franklin also made a strenuous trip to Canada to observe the troops in battle there.

As the American Revolution went on, it became less likely that the colonists and Britain would reach an agreement. Members of the Continental Congress arrived at this conclusion in the summer of 1776. On June 7, a motion was made to draft a statement of independence. Thomas Jefferson, a delegate from Virginia, was selected to draft the first version of the Declaration of Independence. Franklin was asked by Jefferson to

This is a page from Franklin's 1737 ledger, kept when he was deputy postmaster general of Philadelphia. He held this position until 1753. That year he became the first postmaster general of the American colonies, remaining so until 1774.

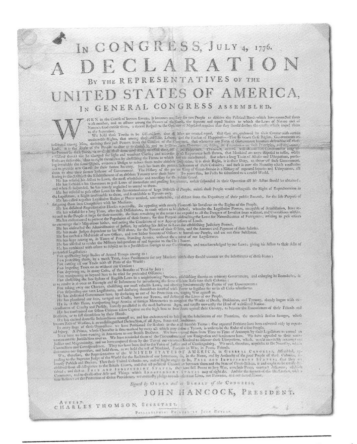

The Declaration of Independence, a document declaring the colonies' independence from Great Britain, was approved by the Second Continental Congress on July 4, 1776. Benjamin Franklin was one of the men who signed and helped to draft this historic document.

review the draft. The Declaration of Independence was adopted on July 4, 1776.

In the summer of 1776, Franklin received a letter from Lord George Howe. Howe had been a friend of Franklin's in London, where they had worked together secretly to find a solution to the tension between the colonies and Britain. Now Howe was in command of the British army in America. Howe wrote to Franklin suggesting the

This portrait of Viscount George Augustus Howe is believed to have been painted between 1723 and 1792. Howe tried to make peace between Britain and the colonies.

colonists would be forgiven if they reaffirmed their loyalty to the British crown.

Franklin turned in the proposition to Congress and asked permission to reply. Franklin wrote a now-famous, personal letter in which he spoke highly of the British Empire and stated how hard he had worked on its behalf. However, Ben Franklin made it clear that no proposal for reconciliation would be accepted. Franklin and the other delegates from Congress again rejected Howe's proposal for reconciliation on September 11, 1776, only this time they did so in a face-to-face meeting.

Shortly afterward, Franklin was selected to join Silas Deane in France to seek support against Britain. On October 27, 1776, a seventy-year-old Franklin sailed for France with his two grandsons, William Temple Franklin and Benjamin Franklin Bache. Franklin wrote to a colleague, "I have only a few years to live, and I am resolved to devote them to the work that my fellow citizens deem proper of me."

Franklin was well received in areas of France such as Paris, where many knew of his reputation as a writer and a scientist. On December 28, 1776, Franklin had his first meeting with the French foreign minister, Charles Gravier, comte de Vergennes. Franklin implied to him that the other countries in Europe would support the colonies against the British. He also implied that if the colonists did not get money and supplies from France, they might be forced to accept reconciliation with Britain.

The colonists found themselves in a bind. France would not commit to the war against Britain unless the colonists showed they could win, but the colonists needed more money and supplies to ensure victory over the British. Things looked even worse for the colonists after the British defeated them in New York and invaded Philadelphia.

Franklin continued to petition the French, and they continued to give funds when necessary. In late 1777, the Continental army scored enough victories for Franklin to convince France to sign a treaty of alliance. The defeat of the British army at Saratoga, New York, especially helped Franklin to win an alliance with France.

Two treaties, or agreements, were made with France in February 1778, and were approved by Louis XVI, king of France, in March. The first was an alliance for mutual defense, and the second was for friendship and commerce. These alliances meant that France would come to the aid of the colonies, and that the colonies would become trading partners with France.

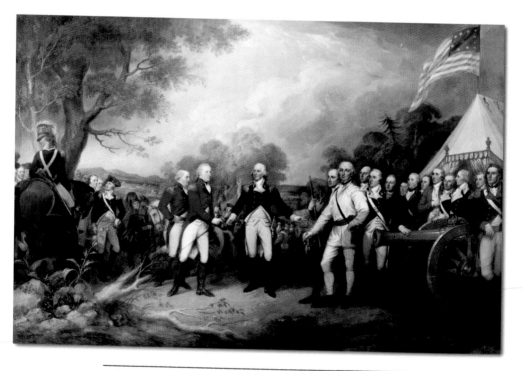

The surrender of British general John Burgoyne at Saratoga, New York, is shown in this 1777 painting by John Trumbull. The Battle of Saratoga was the first great American victory of the American Revolution. France had helped the victory by sending unofficial aid.

9. Negotiations for Peace

The negotiation of an alliance with France took a number of years, and sometimes the biggest obstacles were the American negotiators themselves. Silas Deane was said to be engaged in plans that would make him a profit, rather than in pursuing the interests of the colonies. Arthur Lee, another delegate from America who had worked with Franklin in Britain earlier in his career, was jealous of Franklin and Deane. He often complained of being left out of important negotiations. He hinted at wrongdoings by the other two to Congress. Deane's replacement, the future president John Adams, did not like Franklin very much. The writings of John Adams show both the importance of Franklin to America and Adams's jealousy toward Franklin.

Franklin lived in the town of Passy in the French countryside, so he was not near either government officials or Adams, who were in Paris. Franklin spent much time with academics, philosophers, scientists, and others who came to meet him. He also spent time with his

In 1777, Franklin purchased the equipment to create a small press at the house where he was staying in Passy, France. Franklin coordinated the translation of some of his older writings to French. He also wrote short, humorous essays, known as bagatelles. Franklin wrote several famous bagatelles, one of which consisted of a fake conversation he had with gout, a painful disease of the joints that he was suffering from at the time.

women admirers. As Adams observed, "These visitors occupied all of his time, till it was time to dress and go to dinner. He was invited to dine abroad every day and never declined unless we had invited company to dine with us."

When the colonies signed the alliance with France, there was no longer a need for a three-person delegation in Paris. In September 1778, Franklin was selected to stay in Paris as the minister plenipotentiary to France, or the sole representative of America in France. In this position of minister plenipotentiary, Franklin was forced to deal with some challenging diplomatic situations while continuing to ask France for more money and support for the war effort.

This painting by Baron Jolly shows Franklin at the French court. Benjamin Franklin served from 1776 to 1778 in a three-man group sent to France with the critical job of gaining French support for American independence.

In 1779, Spain joined the war against Britain but refused to recognize American independence. Spain was also trying to take advantage of America by demanding control of the Mississippi River. Franklin responded to John Jay, who was trying to raise money in Spain, by saying, "Poor as we are, yet as I know we shall be rich, I would rather agree with them to buy at a great price the whole of their right on the Mississippi, than sell a drop of its waters. A neighbor might as well ask me to sell my street door."

Other schemes and activities during the war also occupied Franklin's time. He negotiated the release of some American prisoners of war in London while also funding the escape of others. He and John Paul Jones were involved in a plan by Marquis de Lafayette, a well-known French soldier, to attack the British in Liverpool, England—although the plan was later cancelled. Franklin was approached with offers of reconciliation from British spies and diplomats. These offers were always rejected because they did not recognize the independence of the colonies from Britain.

After years of providing just enough money to keep the Continental army running, France finally sent naval support to the colonies in 1781. When General Washington heard that French ships were off the coast of America, he took advantage of this by pinning General Charles Cornwallis and the British army at Yorktown. The British navy was prevented from rescuing British soldiers during the Battle of Yorktown by the French navy. In October 1781, the British surrendered, and the American Revolution was over.

A formal peace treaty was not finalized until September 1783. Benjamin Franklin, John Jay, and John Adams were instrumental in negotiating the treaty. Franklin played a very active role in the negotiations. He also had critics, including Jay and Adams, who thought he was too attached to France to keep the interests of America in mind.

Following British general Cornwallis's defeat at Yorktown, Virginia, Franklin was the only delegate in Paris, France, available to discuss the terms of negotiation and agreement with both Britain and France. Ben Franklin did not have formal instructions from the U.S. Congress but knew that the alliance with France had to be kept at all cost and the colonies' independence had to be recognized.

This 1875 portrait of John Jay is believed to have been based on a portrait of Jay by John Trumbull. Before the American Revolution, Jay opposed British actions but did not favor colonial independence. After the Declaration of Independence was proclaimed, however, Jay energetically supported the patriot cause.

Franklin reminded the British representative, Richard Oswald, that Britain had to negotiate with both America and France at the same time because of their alliance with each other. Ben Franklin also reminded the British representative that America was already independent. The thirteen American colonies had declared their independence in 1776, and they had just won the war. Franklin went on to suggest that Britain give Canada to America as payment for the damages caused by the British against the Americans during the American Revolution.

Franklin drew up a list of negotiating points for Oswald in July 1782. It included necessary items that were not open to negotiation, such as the colonies' complete independence from Britain, an evacuation of all British troops from America, and a determination of boundaries with Canada.

A second list included advisable, or recommended, elements of the treaty. These included cash reparations, or payments for damages and the costs of conducting war, of about half a million pounds, and the turnover of Canada to America. The list also asked for an agreement for free trade without taxes between the two countries. In addition, a formal apology from Britain to America was requested.

The military climate changed in Europe in late 1782. At that point, France began to realize that it might need to work with Britain against other countries in Europe, such as Russia, because of Russia's expansion around the Black Sea. For these reasons, the French government encouraged America to negotiate a peace with Britain that could be separate from France. The new prime minister in London did not want to be associated with the British failure in America, so the peace process sped up.

At the end of 1782, the British were ready to accept the necessary items that Franklin put forth in his proposals. First John Jay and then John Adams joined Franklin in Paris, but most of the negotiating had been done. With Jay's arrival in Paris, Franklin concluded the final details of the drafted peace agreement with Britain. It took almost a year for approval from both Britain and America, but the Treaty of Paris between America and Great Britain was signed on September 3, 1783. The treaty was officially adopted on May 12, 1784.

One reason for the delay was that the Americans did not formally tell the French of the unofficial conditions of the peace agreement. This was a diplomatic issue that upset French foreign minister Vergennes. Franklin apologized to Vergennes for America's poor diplomatic conduct, but reminded the French minister that the agreement was not final.

Franklin's apology and explanation were enough to calm the situation. The two diplomats also realized that Britain would like France and America to end their alliance, and they knew that they could not let this happen. These factors helped Franklin to get French approval for the treaty and to get an additional loan from France to help the Americans pay off the short-term debts they owed from the war.

After the Treaty of Paris was officially adopted, Franklin asked Congress to let him retire. In 1784,

Thomas Jefferson came to Paris to work with Franklin and Adams in negotiating treaties with European nations. In 1785, Franklin requested a replacement. Jefferson was made the minister plenipotentiary to France, and then Congress permitted Franklin to return home.

10. Franklin's Final Years

Franklin might have thought he would never return to Philadelphia after spending so many years in France. Many of his French friends and acquaintances asked him to stay. There were days when Franklin was in so much pain from his gout and kidney stones that he was not sure he could make the trip back to Philadelphia.

In the end, though, Franklin decided to make the trip home. With much ceremony, Franklin set sail for America in July 1785. He would play an important role in the formation of the new American government and would take an active role against slavery.

At age seventy-nine, Franklin made the return voyage to Philadelphia. He made great use of his time by writing *Maritime Observations* during the trip. This publication contained notes on new Gulf Stream observations and many suggestions for improving safety on ships. In September 1785, Franklin landed in Philadelphia and was greeted by large crowds.

Franklin would get little rest. Within a month he was elected to the Supreme Executive Council of

Pennsylvania. He was made president of the council soon afterward. The newly formed state of Pennsylvania did not have formal political parties, but it had two competing groups that wanted Franklin's support. Franklin tried to remain above the differences of the two parties.

Franklin spent much of 1786 getting readjusted to a war-torn Philadelphia that had been occupied by the British at times during the war. Franklin also built a large addition to his house, which included a private library. One of Franklin's final inventions was a wooden "arm" that he created to reach books that were stacked on high shelves.

This 1777 engraving by William Elliott depicts naval action in the Delaware River off the coast of Philadelphia.

In the beginning of 1787, Franklin was named president of the Pennsylvania Society for Promoting the Abolition of Slavery. His views on slavery had developed over many years, as had the views of many other Americans of the time. Despite having been a slave owner, toward the end of his life, Franklin would play an active role in the movement to abolish slavery.

It was not until 1748, when he was forty years old, that Franklin acquired his first slaves. In 1763, Franklin visited a school for blacks run by a charitable organization in Philadelphia. Franklin wrote about his visit and remarked that he "conceived a higher opinion of the natural capabilities of the Black Race than I had ever before entertained." It was not until 1772, however, that Franklin wrote an article against the slave trade called "The Somerset Case and the Slave Trade." It was against the practice of capturing black people in Africa and shipping them to be sold as slaves in the colonies and in Europe. In the article, Franklin did not go so far as to condemn slavery as morally wrong.

In 1787, Franklin finally began to take steps in speaking out against slavery. For the few remaining years of his life, Franklin would dedicate much of his efforts to ending the institution of slavery. In 1789, Franklin wrote and signed a public address stating that slavery was "an atrocious debasement of human nature." Franklin also made several proposals in Congress for the abolition of slavery and the education of slaves. In 1790, the last year of his life, Franklin again petitioned Congress to put an end to slavery and the slave trade.

Franklin was the elder statesman of the new country and was very involved at the Constitutional Convention that began in Philadelphia in 1787. Many people believed the Articles of Confederation that currently governed the new country gave the states too much power. Every state had its own set of institutions and practices, which made cooperation difficult and threatened the stability of the new country.

The Constitutional Convention was called to create a stronger central or federal government. The biggest challenge the delegates faced was determining how the states and the voters would be represented. Franklin thought that there should be an executive council rather than one president along with just one group of representatives. Other delegates felt it best to have two separate lawmaking groups in the federal government.

The result of the debates was known as the Great Compromise, and Franklin had a role in the first proposals for a solution. The final compromise was that there would be two legislative houses: the Senate and the House of Representatives. The Senate would have equal representation, two senators per state, no matter the size of the state. The senators were to be chosen by the state legislative bodies. Population, or the number of people in the states, would determine the number of votes each state received in the other legislative body, the House of Representatives.

On the issue of the executive office, Franklin had proposed an executive council. Others, such as Alexander Hamilton, proposed that there be just one executive. The result of this compromise was that there would be a single executive, the president, who could only be in office for a limited term of four years.

The delegates rejected Franklin's proposal to start each session of the convention with a prayer. Some delegates wanted to restrict the right to vote to those who owned large amounts of land. This view went against what Franklin wanted. Franklin did not go so far as to suggest that voting be extended to women, blacks, and the poor, but he did want to give more people the right to vote.

When the compromises were worked out, delegates were still not quite satisfied. Franklin's closing address asked those in the convention to be active in support of the Constitution when presenting it to the voters in the states. The Constitution was sent out to the states for ratification, or official approval, in September 1787.

There were many obstacles to overcome before the Constitution would be approved by the states. Some Americans did not want such a strong federal government. Others did not want the individual states to be too powerful. Franklin wrote an influential piece that supported the Constitution in a newspaper article.

Alexander Hamilton (1755–1804), the first secretary of the
U.S. Treasury, is known for his role in settling the finances of the
American Revolution and for his advocacy of a strong central
government for the new United States.

With the help of Franklin's support and arguments, the U.S. Constitution was officially ratified in 1788.

The ratification of the Constitution occurred at the same time that Franklin was retiring from public life. By 1788, Franklin had served as president of the Executive Council of Pennsylvania for as many terms as were allowed by law. His retirement and rest were accompanied by the ailments and pains of old age. Franklin remained active in the antislavery movement even as he withdrew from public office. During this time Franklin continued to write letters to colleagues about science and many other ideas.

11. The Legacy of Benjamin Franklin

After years of suffering from gout, kidney stones, and other sicknesses brought on by age, Franklin died at home in Philadelphia on April 17, 1790, at age eighty-four. The life of America's greatest inventor, writer, and patriot had come to an end. On April 21, 1790, Benjamin Franklin was buried next to his wife, Deborah, and their son Francis at the Christ Church burial ground.

Franklin's death was met by mourning on both sides of the Atlantic Ocean. In Philadelphia, about half of the city, or 20,000 people, attended the funeral procession. Congress also unanimously declared a day of mourning. In France, members of the assembly wore black and speeches were given in Franklin's honor.

The lasting importance of Benjamin Franklin's life can still be seen today in many different ways. The name Franklin, like the name of Washington and other patriots, is widely used in the naming of streets, towns, and schools. Franklin's legacy is also evident in the clubs and the organizations he formed, which have become the

As a young printer,
Franklin had taken the time
to write his own epitaph,
which incorporated some
of his thoughts on life and religion:

The Body of
B. Franklin,
Printer;
Like the Cover of an old Book,
Its contents torn out,
And stript of its Lettering and Gilding,
Lies here, Food for Worms,
But the Work shall not be wholly lost,
For it will, as he believed, appear once more,
In a new & more perfect Edition,
Corrected and amended
By the Author.

This 1853 engraving shows the site of Benjamin Franklin's grave at Christ Church in Philadelphia, Pennsylvania. He was buried beside his wife, Deborah, who had died twenty-five years before Franklin. Franklin's son Francis Folger, who had died at age four from smallpox, is also buried in the family plot.

libraries, police forces, and fire companies of today. Franklin's study of electricity and other scientific observations were very important in the electrical revolution that followed. Of Franklin's many inventions, those still in use today include lightning rods and bifocal glasses.

During the final years of his life, Franklin took the time to send out his autobiography to his friends for review. Franklin was looking back on his life and thinking about his own image. He shaped stories in the book to make himself look good. Franklin also added morals, or lessons, he learned later in life to events that had happened to him earlier. Still, when the *Autobiography* was published, it was the first account of its kind. Today many students read *The Autobiography of Benjamin Franklin* in American schools.

Because of Franklin's tireless dedication to the American cause, he is remembered as a patriot. His work as an American patriot was instrumental in the formation of the United States of America. Franklin was the only American to be involved in the creation of the Declaration of Independence, the alliance with France, the peace treaty with Britain, and the Constitution of the United States. This accomplishment does not even take into account his work for the people of Pennsylvania before and after the American Revolution, and his activism against slavery.

As a writer, a philosopher, a scientist, and an inventor, his legacy is equally secure. His writings as Poor Richard were translated into many languages and were read throughout Europe even in his own time. The words of wisdom and moral lessons in his almanacs are still quoted today. Many people, when they think of Franklin's electrical experiments, remember only Franklin flying a kite in a thunderstorm. However, his numerous experiments in electricity advanced this field of study by many years.

When we think of all that Franklin was able to accomplish, despite his faults and failures, we see his

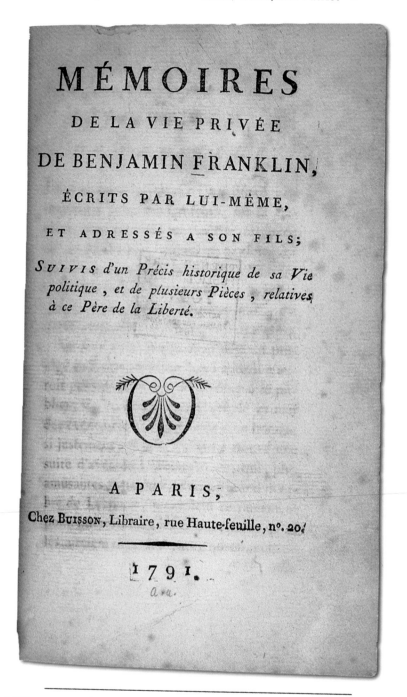

In 1791, a year after Benjamin Franklin's death, his autobiography was published in French, in Paris. The first English translation was published in London in 1793. The book, originally written for Franklin's son William, offers observations about literature, philosophy, and religion.

life as a truly remarkable one. Benjamin Franklin's accomplishments and outlook on life made him one of the most important founding fathers of America, and the most famous American of his time. The contributions of this son of a Boston working man, who built his own business and became a world-renowned inventor and writer, make Franklin perhaps one of the most eminent Americans of all time.

Timeline

1706   Benjamin Franklin is born on January 17, in Boston, Massachusetts.

1718   Franklin becomes a printer's apprentice to his brother James.

1722   Franklin begins writing his Silence Dogood letters.

1723   Franklin sails to Philadelphia and begins his job as a printer.

1730   Franklin becomes the official printer for Pennsylvania's government.

           In September, Franklin and Deborah Read join into a common-law marriage.

1732   In December, Franklin publishes the first *Poor Richard's Almanack*.

1737   Franklin starts his job as postmaster of Philadelphia.

1750   Franklin proposes the experiment to prove lightning is electricity.

1751   In May, Franklin is elected to the

Pennsylvania assembly.

1752 In June, it is thought that Franklin develops and performs the kite experiment.

1753 In August, he is appointed the deputy postmaster of the colonies.

1755 Franklin works with the Quaker Party in demanding that the Penn family—the proprietors of Pennsylvania—pay taxes on their lands.

1757 In February, Franklin leaves for London to petition the government for assistance in making the Penns pay taxes on land for defense.

1765 In February, Franklin and the colonies protest the proposed Stamp Act. However, the Stamp Act is passed.

1766 In February, the Stamp Act is removed.

1770 On March 5, the Boston Massacre occurs.

1773 On December 16, the Boston Tea Party occurs.

1775 In March, Franklin leaves London after Massachusetts is declared in rebellion.

1776 In June, Franklin reviews the

Declaration of Independence, which is adopted on July 4.

1781   The U.S. Congress appoints Franklin, John Jay, John Adams, Thomas Jefferson, and Henry Laurens to negotiate a peace settlement with Britain.

1782   Between March and June, informal peace negotiations with Britain begin between Franklin and Richard Oswald.

1784   In May, a peace treaty between America and Britain is officially signed.

1787   In April, Franklin is elected president of the Pennsylvania Society for Promoting the Abolition of Slavery.

1790   On April 17, Benjamin Franklin dies in Philadelphia at the age of 84.

Glossary

allied (A-lyd) In close association with another.

almanac (AHL-meh-nak) A book of general information, including weather predictions; usually used by farmers to help them plant and harvest crops.

American Revolution (uh-MER-uh-ken reh-vuh-LOO-shun) The war American colonists fought from 1775 to 1783 to win independence from Britain.

apprentice (uh-PREN-tis) A person who works for another to learn a trade.

Articles of Confederation (AR-tih-kuls UV kun-feh-duh-RAY-shun) The laws that governed the United States before the Constitution was created.

bagatelles (ba-guh-TELZ) Short pieces of writing that Franklin wrote while in France; in general, trifles.

braziers (BRA-zherz) People who work with brass.

civic (SIH-vik) Relating to citizens or to people who are part of a society.

colonial (kuh-LOH-nee-ul) Having to do with the period of time when the United States was made of thirteen colonies ruled by Britain.

common-law marriage (KAH-min LAW MEHR-ij) A marriage recognized in some places and based on the parties' agreement to consider themselves married; also a marriage based on two people living together.

confederation (kun-feh-duh-RAY-shun) A loosely united group of people, organizations, or governments.

delegates (DEH-lih-gets) People who present ideas on behalf of many other people.

diplomat (DIH-pleh-mat) 1. The representative of a country. 2. Someone who conducts talks between nations.

doctorates (DOK-ter-its) Degrees or titles of a doctor.

executive (eg-ZEH-kyuh-tiv) Belonging to the branch of government that manages the affairs of a nation and sees that the laws are carried out.

federal (FEH-deh-rul) A form of government in which power is distributed between a central authority and a number of states.

French and Indian War (FRENCH AND IN-dee-un WOR) The battles fought between 1754 and 1763 by Britain, France, and Native American allies for control of North America.

gout (GOWT) A disease that affects the joints.

grounded (GROWND-ed) To make an electrical connection with the earth.

illegitimate (il-leh-JIH-tih-miht) Not beng done in the proper way, such as a child being born out of wedlock.

Iroquois Confederacy (EER-ih-kwoy kon-FEH-duh-ruh-see) A Native American group that lived in New York State and originally was composed of five different nations.

joiners (JOY-nerz) People whose occupation is to make objects by joining pieces of wood.

journeyman (JER-nee-man) A worker who learned a trade from one person, but who works for another.

legislative (LEH-jus-lay-tiv) The branch of the government that makes laws and collects taxes.

mentor (MEN-tor) A person who provides leadership and guidance, and serves as a role model for another.

minister plenipotentiary (MIN-is-tur pleh-neh-puh-TEN-shuh-ree) A diplomatic agent who ranks below an ambassador but has full power.

moralist (MOR-uh-list) A philosopher or a writer who is concerned with moral issues, that is teaching people to understand the difference between right and wrong behavior.

petition (puh-TIH-shun) A document signed by many people that requests a specific action by a group or a government.

postmaster general (POST-mas-ter JEN-rul) The

official in charge of a national post office or agency.

Puritan (PYUR-ih-tin) People in the 1500s and the 1600s who belonged to a strict sect of the Protestant religion.

reparations (reh-puh-RAY-shunz) The payment required from a defeated nation to pay for the damages it caused during a war to the winning nation.

smallpox (SMAL-poks) A severe, contagious disease characterized by blisters and scar formation.

statesman (STAYTS-mun) A political leader who conducts government business and shapes policies.

tallow chandler (TAH-loh CHAND-ler) A maker of candles out of melted sheep or cattle fat.

Treaty of Paris (TREE-tee UV PAR-es) The name of several important peace agreements signed at or near Paris that ended the American Revolution.

turners (TER-nerz) People who form articles with a lathe, a woodworking tool.

U.S. Constitution (YOO ES kahn-stih-TOO-shun) The basic rules by which the United States is run.

wedlock (WED-lok) The state of being married.

Additional Resources

To learn more about Benjamin Franklin, check out
these books and Web sites:

Books

Adler, David. *A Picture of Benjamin Franklin*. New
York: Holiday House, 1990.

Cousins, Margaret. *Ben Franklin of Old Philadelphia*.
New York: Random House, 1980.

Davidson, Margaret. *The Story of Benjamin Franklin,
Amazing American*. New York: Bantam Doubleday
Dell Books, 1988.

Fritz, Jean. *What's the Big Idea, Ben Franklin?* New
York: Penguin Putnam Books, 1976.

Gross, Ruth Belov. *A Book About Benjamin Franklin*.
Scholastic: New York, 1975.

Wright, E. ed. *The Sayings of Benjamin Franklin*.
London: Redwood Books, 1995.

Web Sites

Due to the changing nature of Internet links, Power Plus
Books has developed an online list of Web sites related to
the subject of this book. This site is updated regularly.
Please use this link to access the list:
www.powerkidslinks.com/lalt/franklin/

Bibliography

Brands, H. W. *The First American: The Life and Times of Benjamin Franklin*. New York: Doubleday, 2000.

Franklin, Benjamin. *Autobiography of Benjamin Franklin*. Mineola, New York: Dover Publications, 1996.

Franklin, Benjamin. *Benjamin Franklin: Writings*. Lemay, J. A. Leo., ed. New York: Library of Congress, 1987.

Franklin, Benjamin. *Poor Richard's Almanack*. Paul Leicester Ford, ed. Mount Vernon, New York: Peter Pauper Press, 1936.

Van Doren, Carl. *Benjamin Franklin*. New York: Penguin Books, 1939.

Primary Resources:

Benjamin Franklin Collection, American Philosophical Society (Philadelphia, Pennsylvania)

Benjamin Franklin Collection, Yale University (New Haven, Connecticut)

The Franklin Institute Science Museum

The Papers of Benjamin Franklin, Leonard W. Labaree, et al. (New Haven, Connecticut, 1959–present)

Index

About the Author

Ryan P. Randolph is a freelance writer with an avid interest in history. Ryan has a Bachelor of Arts degree in both history and political science from Colgate University in Hamilton, New York. Ryan is also a member of the history honor society Phi Alpha Theta. He has written several history books for children. He currently works in a financial consulting firm and lives with his wife in New York.

Credits

Photo Credits

Cover: Independence National Historic Park (portrait); Library of Congress Prints and Photographs Division (painting). Pp. 4, 8, 83, 92 Independence National Historic Park; pp. 7, 44 Franklin Institute; pp. 9, 78 Architect of the Capitol; pp. 12, 21, 36, 53 © Bettmann/CORBIS; pp. 13, 18 Dover Pictorial Archive Series; pp. 14, 50 Culver Pictures; pp. 21, 34, 62, 73 Library of Congress Prints and Photographs Division; pp. 22 Library of Congress, Geography and Map Division, Washington, D.C.; pp. 23, 39 Courtesy of the Historical of Pennsylvania Society, (Society Collection); pp. 26, 74 the American Philosophical Society; p. 29 Courtesy of Map Division, The New York Public Library, Astor, Lenox and Tilden Foundations; p. 33 Courtesy of the Library Company of Philadelphia; p. 35 Reproduced with permission from the Robert H. Gore, Jr. Numismatic Collection, Department of Special Collections, University of Notre Dame Libraries; p. 40 Cigna Museum and Art Collection; p. 45 created by Corinne Jacob; p. 46 From Collection of Historical Scientific Instruments Harvard University, Cambridge, Massachusetts; p. 49 © Museum of the City of New York/CORBIS; pp. 50, 68 North Wind; pp. 52, 55, 96 © CORBIS; p. 58 From the Collection of Gilcrease Museum, Tulsa, OK; p. 61 © The Corcoran Gallery of Art/CORBIS; p. 64 © Lee Snider; Lee Snider/ CORBIS; p. 70 Print Collection, Miriam and Ira D. Wallach Division of Art, Prints and Photographs, The New York Public Library, Astor, Lenox and Tilden Foundations; p. 75 National Archives and Records Administration; p. 76 Christie's Images, Ltd. 2001; p. 81 Philadelphia Museum of Art: Gift of Graeme and Sarah Lorimer in memory of their granddaughter, Mary Caroline Morris; p. 88 the Phelps Stokes Collection, Miriam and Ira D. Wallach Division of Art, Prints, and Photographs, the New York Public Library, Astor, Lenox, and Tilden Foundations; p. 98 Rare Books and Manuscripts, New York Public Library, Astor, Lenox, and Tilden Foundations.

Editor
Leslie Kaplan

Series Design
Laura Murawski

Layout Design
Corinne Jacob

Photo Researcher
Jeffrey Wendt